SOUTH AMERICA
TODAY

VENEZUELA

SOUTH AMERICA
TODAY

VENEZUELA

Charles J. Shields

Mason Crest Publishers
Philadelphia

Produced by OTTN Publishing, Stockton, N.J.

Mason Crest Publishers
370 Reed Road
Broomall, PA 19008
www.masoncrest.com

First printing

1 3 5 7 9 8 6 4 2

Library of Congress Cataloging-in-Publication Data

Shields, Charles J., 1951-
  Venezuela / Charles J. Shields.
      p. cm. — (South America today)
    ISBN 978-1-4222-0643-0 (hardcover) — ISBN 978-1-4222-0710-9 (pbk.)
  1. Venezuela—Juvenile literature. [1. Venezuela.] I. Title.
  F2308.5.S55 2008
  987—dc22
                                        2008032322

SOUTH AMERICA TODAY

Argentina
Bolivia
Brazil
Chile
Colombia

South America:
Facts & Figures
Ecuador
Guyana

Paraguay
Peru
Suriname
Uruguay
Venezuela

Table of Contents

Discovering South America

James D. Henderson

South America is a cornucopia of natural resources, a treasure house of ecological variety. It is also a continent of striking human diversity and geographic extremes. Yet in spite of that, most South Americans share a set of cultural similarities. Most of the continent's inhabitants are properly termed "Latin" Americans. This means that they speak a Romance language (one closely related to Latin), particularly Spanish or Portuguese. It means, too, that most practice Roman Catholicism and share the Mediterranean cultural patterns brought by the Spanish and Portuguese who settled the continent over five centuries ago.

Still, it is never hard to spot departures from these cultural norms. Bolivia, Peru, and Ecuador, for example, have significant Indian populations who speak their own languages and follow their own customs. In Paraguay the main Indian language, Guaraní, is accepted as official along with Spanish. Nor are all South Americans Catholics. Today Protestantism is making steady gains, while in Brazil many citizens practice African religions right along with Catholicism and Protestantism.

South America is a lightly populated continent, having just 6 percent of the world's people. It is also the world's most tropical continent, for a larger percentage of its land falls between the tropics of Cancer and Capricorn than is the case with any other continent. The world's driest desert is there, the Atacama in northern Chile, where no one has ever seen a drop of rain fall. And the world's wettest place is there too, the Chocó region of Colombia, along that country's border with Panama. There it rains almost every day. South America also has some of the world's highest mountains, the Andes,

Evening in Caracas, Venezuela's capital and largest city.

and its greatest river, the Amazon.

So welcome to South America! Through this colorfully illustrated series of books you will travel through 12 countries, from giant Brazil to small Suriname. On your way you will learn about the geography, the history, the economy, and the people of each one. Geared to the needs of teachers and students, each volume contains book and web sources for further study, a chronology, project and report ideas, and even recipes of tasty and easy-to-prepare dishes popular in the countries studied. Each volume describes the country's national holidays and the cities and towns where they are held. And each book is indexed.

You are embarking on a voyage of discovery that will take you to lands not so far away, but as interesting and exotic as any in the world.

Venezuela has a wide range of geographical regions and climates—tall mountains, sandy beaches, swampy lowlands, and green plateaus. (Opposite) The beach at Península de Paraguaná. (Right) The verdant landscape near Mérida.

1 An Exotic Land

CHRISTOPHER COLUMBUS described Venezuela as a paradise. Shaped roughly like an upside-down triangle, the country has a coastline 1,740 miles (2,800 kilometers) long that is bounded on the north by the Caribbean Sea and the Atlantic Ocean. Venezuela's neighbors are Guyana to the east, Brazil to the south, and Colombia to the west.

Venezuela has white sand beaches and clear water, dry and desert-like zones, and beautiful giant plateaus called *tepuíes*. Naturalists as well as tourists seek out the unusual plants and animals found on the *tepuíes*, in the dense green of Venezuela's jungles, and at the foot of the Andes Mountains.

Lowlands, Mountains, Plains, Highlands

Venezuela has four fairly well defined regions: the Maracaibo Lowlands in the northwest; the northern mountains that arc from the Colombian border along the Caribbean Sea; the wide Orinoco River plains in central Venezuela; and the broken-up Guiana Highlands in the southeast.

The Maracaibo Lowlands form a large, spoon-shaped oval surrounded by mountains on three sides, but open on the north to the Caribbean Sea. The area is very flat with only a gentle slope toward the center and away from the mountains. Lago de Maracaibo (Lake Maracaibo) occupies much of the lower-lying territory. Areas around the southern part of Lago de Maracaibo are swampy. Some *palafito* villages ("villages in the lake") like Ceuta and San Timoteo are built on piers above the water. Farmers and fishers work along the banks.

The northern mountains bordering the Caribbean Sea are an extension of the Andes Mountains. Broken by several gaps, these high mountains have peaks over 14,750 feet (4,500 meters) tall. To the west, an irregular range runs along the Colombian border. Some of Venezuela's highest peaks rise here, southeast of Lago de Maracaibo. A few are snowcapped year-round, among them Pico Bolívar, the highest peak in the country, which reaches 16,427 feet (5,007 meters). A wide gap separates this mountainous area from another rugged pair of ranges that run parallel to the north-central coast.

Between these two ranges are a group of valleys that make up the economic heartland of Venezuela. This area, where the capital city, Caracas, is located, has the country's densest population, the most productive agriculture, and the best transportation network. Venezuela's eastern region is dotted with broken hills and uplands, which rise steeply from the Caribbean and stretch eastward almost to the island of Trinidad.

The vast lowlands, which were formed over many centuries by the flow of the Orinoco River, run westward from the Caribbean coast to the Colombian border between the northern mountains and the Orinoco River. This region is known as *Los Llanos* (the Plains), although it also contains large stretches of swampland in the Orinoco Delta and the region near the Colombian border. The area slopes gradually away from the highland areas that surround it. Elevations in the llanos never exceed 656 feet (200 meters). North of the Río Apure, a **tributary** of the Orinoco, rivers flowing out of the northern mountains cut shallow valleys, leaving eroded ridges that give the land a gently rolling appearance. South of the Apure, the terrain is flatter and the elevations are lower.

The Guiana Highlands, which cover

A stream runs through the forest near Jaji, a small town high in the Andes Mountains.

Quick Facts: The Geography of Venezuela

Location: Northern South America, bordering the Caribbean Sea and the North Atlantic Ocean, between Colombia and Guyana

Area: (slightly more than twice the size of California)
  total: 352,142 square miles (912,050 sq km)
  land: 340,559 square miles (882,050 sq km)
  water: 11,583 square miles (30,000 sq km)

Borders: Brazil, 1,367 miles (2,200 km); Colombia, 1,274 miles (2,050 km); Guyana, 462 miles (743 km)

Climate: tropical; hot, humid; more moderate in highlands

Terrain: Andes Mountains and Maracaibo Lowlands in the northwest; central plains (llanos); Guiana Highlands in the southeast

Elevation extremes:
  lowest point: Caribbean Sea—0 feet
  highest point: Pico Bolívar—16,427 feet (5,007 meters)

Natural hazards: floods, rockslides, mudslides, periodic droughts

Source: Adapted from CIA World Factbook, 2002.

almost half the country, suddenly rise south and east of the Orinoco River. Erosion has created strange formations here. The highlands are mainly plateaus cut into pieces by running tributaries of the Orinoco. The most eye-catching plateau is the Gran Sabana, a giant, deeply eroded formation that rises from surrounding areas as a collection of steep cliffs. Above the rolling surface of the Gran Sabana, massive, flat-topped *tepuíes* emerge. The world's highest waterfall, Angel Falls, tumbles over one of these *tepuíes*.

The Water System of Venezuela

The Orinoco is by far the most important of the more than 1,000 rivers in Venezuela. It flows more than 1,554 miles (2,500 km) to the Atlantic from its source in the Guiana Highlands at the Brazilian border. The Orinoco is the world's eighth-largest river and the second-largest in South America (after the Amazon). Its depth and the speed of its current change with the seasons. In August, for example, the Orinoco is 40 feet (12 meters) higher than it is in March and April.

Downstream from its *headwaters*, the Orinoco splits into two. One-third of its flow passes through the Brazo Casiquiare (Casiquiare Channel) into a tributary of the Amazon, and the rest passes into the main Orinoco channel.

Most of the rivers rising in the northern mountains flow southeastward to the Río Apure. From its headwaters, the Apure crosses the llanos in a generally eastward direction. Few rivers flow into it from the poorly drained region south of the river. Much of the region near the Colombian border is swampland.

The other major Venezuelan river is the fast-flowing Caroní, which starts in the Guiana Highlands and flows northward into the Orinoco at a spot upstream from Ciudad Guayana. The Caroní is capable of producing as much hydroelectric power as any river in Latin America and has contributed significantly to the nation's electric power production.

Lago de Maracaibo, the largest lake in Latin America, occupies the central 5,212 square miles (13,500 sq km) of the Maracaibo Lowlands. Beneath its shore and the lake floor lie most of Venezuela's rich petroleum deposits. The lake is shallow, with an average depth of 30 feet (9 meters), and it is separated from the Caribbean by a series of islands and *sandbars*. A channel cuts through the sandbars to allow shipping between the lake and the Caribbean. Unfortunately, the channel also allows saltwater to mix with the yellowish freshwater of the lake, making the northern end of it *brackish* and unsuitable for drinking or irrigation.

Temperature Depends on Elevation and Winds

Although Venezuela lies wholly within the Tropics, its climate varies from tropical humid to *alpine*, depending on the elevation and the direction of the winds. In contrast to the United States and many other countries, Venezuela has only two seasons, and they are marked by changes in rainfall instead of temperature. Most of the country has a rainy season (May through November), which is winter. The period between December and April is summer.

Differences in elevation create four temperature zones in Venezuela. In the tropical zone, which is below 2,620 feet (800 meters), temperatures are hot, with yearly averages ranging between 79°F and 82°F (26°C to 28°C). The temperate zone ranges between 2,600 and 6,550 feet (790 and 2,000 meters), with averages from 54°F to 78°F (12°C to 25°C). Many of Venezuela's cities, including the capital, lie in this region. Colder conditions are found in the zone between 6,550 and 9,850 feet (2,000 and 3,000 meters). Here average temperatures range from 48°F to 52°F (9°C to 11°C). In areas higher than 9,850 feet (3,000 meters), cool pastureland and snowy mountainsides have yearly averages below 48°F (9°C).

Average annual rainfall in the lowlands and plains varies from close to 17 inches (43 centimeters) in the *semiarid* western part of the Caribbean coastal areas to around 39 inches (100 cm) in the Orinoco Delta. In the mountains, different locations receive different amounts of rainfall. Sheltered valleys receive little rain, but mountain slopes exposed to the northeast *trade winds* receive heavy rainfall. Caracas averages 30 inches (75 cm) of precipitation annually, more than half of it falling from June through August.

Tropical to Mountain Vegetation

Because of its wide range of elevations and climates, Venezuela has many different types of vegetation. Some two-fifths of the country is covered

A variety of vegetation can be found in Venezuela. (Left) Cacti and other desert plants thrive on the Península de Paraguaná. (Below) Coconut palms can be found along the country's long coastline.

with forests; another half, with *savanna* grasses. Less than 5 percent of the total land is farmland, found mostly in the valleys of the coastal ranges and the Andes.

Tropical vegetation in the lowlands changes to tall savanna grasslands as the elevation rises. Semitropical plants like ferns and orchids continue to grow in areas below 5,000 feet (1,525 meters). Higher up the Andean slopes, this fern forest gives way to mountain vegetation, which features few trees but a variety of small alpine shrubs and mosses. The drier northwestern coastal area was once covered with dry scrub woodland and grasses. But excessive clearing and farming has exposed the soil to erosion.

Jaguars, Boa Constrictors, and Piranha!

The animals of Venezuela belong to South American species found throughout the northern tropical forest and savanna areas of the continent. Seven species of the cat family inhabit the forested interior, including the jaguar, ocelot, jaguarundi, puma, and margay. Several monkey species live in forested territories, among them the howler and spider monkey, the long-tailed capuchin, and the nocturnal durukuli. Other forest animals include wild dog, South American rodents, such as the agouti and the skunk, and various species of bear, peccary, deer, and opossum. Among the more unusual breeds are the tapir, a squat, big-nosed, split-hoofed mammal; and the *aquatic*, plant-eating manatee, which resembles the walrus. The Gran Sabana National Reserve has an amazing array of wildlife.

Living in the less traveled rivers, coastal lagoons, and swamps are several reptilians, including alligators and caimans (a tropical species related to the alligator), lizards, and several species of turtle. Many species of snake, too, inhabit the forested interior, including the venomous coral snake, the striped rattlesnake, and the bushmaster, as well as such nonpoisonous types as the boa constrictor and anaconda.

Birds are plentiful and diverse. The coastal swamps are stopovers for migratory cranes, herons, storks, and ducks. The ibis, a bird similar to the heron, colonizes the mangrove swamps of the Orinoco Delta.

Sharks and coral fish live off the Caribbean coast and in the offshore waters of the Orinoco River. In Venezuela's rivers and streams are mollusks, freshwater shrimp, electric eels, and piranha. Catfish is a popular fish to catch for food.

(Opposite) A statue of Simón Bolívar (1783–1830) in Mérida. Bolívar was a key figure in Venezuela's history; he led revolts against the Spanish in South America during the early 19th century. (Right) During 2002, opposition to the policies of Venezuela's president, Hugo Chávez, led to street protests; a general strike paralyzed the nation at the end of the year.

2 A Late Bloomer in South American History

VENEZUELA NEVER WAS as pivotal to Spain's colonial empire as other colonies of the Americas because it lacked gold, silver, and precious stones. The Spanish were unaware of the value of oil; they called the *petroleum* that oozed out of the ground "the devil's excrement." Eventually, cocoa became the country's principal export. The petroleum industry, which began in the 1930s, eventually replaced cocoa. Since then, Venezuela's history has been strongly shaped by the ups and downs of the oil market.

The Garden of Eden

The first Venezuelans lived in the region between 13,000 and 6,000 B.C. These settlers belonged to different *Amerindian* tribes. Some were farmers,

19

hunters, and fishers. Others were warriors who traveled in wooden boats. All the communities were built to suit the climate and their ways of life.

Christopher Columbus first sighted Venezuela during his third voyage to the New World. On August 1, 1498, he became the first European to walk on the South American mainland. Thinking he had landed on an island, he christened the territory Isla de García. He spent the following weeks exploring the Orinoco Delta. Columbus was delighted by the freshwater rivers and pools, and by the pearl ornaments the native people wore. He believed that he had discovered the biblical Garden of Eden.

A second Spanish expedition followed just one year later. Commanded by Alonso de Ojeda, a Spaniard, and Amerigo Vespucci, from Florence, Italy, the ships sailed westward along the coast as far as Lago de Maracaibo. There they saw the native huts of the *palafitos* built above the lakes. These reminded Vespucci of Venice, a city of canals in his native Italy. He renamed the land Venezuela, or Little Venice.

At first, pearls and rumors of precious metals drew more Spanish expeditions to Venezuela. But by the 1520s, the limited supply of oysters (which create pearls) had nearly run out. The Spanish then realized that they could make their wealth using Venezuelan natives as slaves.

Slave raiding began in the Península de Paria, on the northeast coast. Gradually, the raiders moved inland to capture unwary natives. Slave ships transported thousands of prisoners to the Spanish gold and silver mines in Panama and the Caribbean islands. For years, the native people fought back. But there was no strong leader to unite them, and their villages, towns, and culture eventually disappeared at the hands of the conquerors.

The slave trade tapered off when the Spanish throne sold control of the coast to a group of German bankers in 1528. For the next 28 years, mining companies financed by the German banks tracked down rumors of fabulous gold cities and treasures. Inland peoples fled to avoid being captured or killed. By 1556, when no riches were discovered, Spain ended its contract with the bankers.

Meanwhile, Spanish explorers used the rivers to penetrate deeper into the country, founding a city in 1555 that would eventually become Valencia. After more than a decade of fierce fighting against the natives, Spanish soldiers under Diego de Losada established another settlement, Santiago de León de Caracas, in 1567. Caracas soon became important because it was easily reached from the coast by a passage through the mountains.

The interior plains went mostly unexplored. The Spanish instead fortified the coast as a stopover for their ships, which crossed the Caribbean loaded with gold and silver from settlements in Mexico, Peru, and Panama.

Under the Spanish, Venezuela had no political unity. It was considered a minor colony because it produced few precious metals. Farms and ranches spread into the Andean region and the western plains. But to the Spanish rulers, exports of wheat, tobacco, cocoa, and leather were not very interesting. Venezuelans sold most of their agricultural goods to British, French, or Dutch traders.

The Cocoa Boom

Cocoa became Venezuela's principal export in the 1620s. It would remain the country's most important product for the next two centuries. The cocoa bean is used to make chocolate, which the natives of South America prized. Spanish *conquistadors* discovered chocolate during their conquests of Mexico and took the substance back to their home country, where it soon became very popular.

Cocoa farming had a great impact on colonial Venezuela. To be profitable, cocoa plantations needed an inexpensive source of labor. At first, Native Americans were pressed into service, but many soon died from disease or harsh treatment. During the 17th and 18th centuries the Spanish plantation owners imported slaves from Africa to meet their labor needs.

As a result, over the years Venezuela became a society divided into social layers by skin color. At the top, holding much of the power, were whites from Spain (*peninsulares*) or whites born to Spanish families in Venezuela (*criollos*). Next came *mestizos*, or people of mixed Spanish-Amerindian descent. Blacks and Native Americans were at the bottom of the pecking order. By the early 19th century the native population represented less than 10 percent of Venezuela's population.

In 1811 the Venezuelan congress took advantage of a period of disorder in Europe. The previous year, the French emperor Napoleon Bonaparte had unseated the Spanish royal family and placed his brother on the throne. On December 21, 1811, Venezuelan leaders ratified a constitution that marked the official beginning of Venezuela's First Republic. Known commonly by Venezuelan historians as La Patria Boba (the Silly Republic), it was badly run by privileged Spanish families. The task of overturning La Patria Boba and establishing a better government fell to the leading hero of Latin America's struggle for independence, Simón Bolívar.

Bolívar the Liberator

Bolívar was born in 1783; his family was one of Caracas's wealthiest. After he was orphaned at age nine, relatives took him to Europe, where he was educated. As a young man, Bolívar declared his ambition to unite and liberate from Spanish rule not only his native Venezuela, but all of Latin America. In 1813 he vowed to force Venezuela's Spanish rulers out; with his troops he marched over the Andes to capture Caracas. There he was proclaimed "the Liberator," and following the establishment of the Second Republic, he was given complete power as a dictator.

But after King Ferdinand VII regained control of Spain in late 1814, he fought the South American resistance more aggressively, and his forces

Francisco Miranda (1750–1816) and other Venezuelan leaders sign the declaration of independence from Spain on July 5, 1811. Miranda, a member of Venezuela's *criollo* elite, was the early leader of the independence movement. But other *criollos* refused to give him enough power to govern the First Republic effectively. In 1812 he surrendered his army to Spain; he ultimately died in a Spanish prison.

crushed the remaining Venezuelan troops. Bolívar had no choice but to flee to Jamaica. He returned five years later at the head of a volunteer army that included European recruits. Bolívar quickly marched his troops across the llanos and into the Andes. In a surprise attack on the garrison at Boyacá, near Bogotá, Bolívar's troops defeated the Spaniards and liberated the area that is modern-day Colombia (then called New Granada).

In June 1821, Bolívar's troops fought the Battle of Carabobo. Their decisive victory freed Caracas from Spanish rule. Bolívar, however, continued fighting to liberate South America from Spain's empire, leading his forces against the Spanish strongholds in Ecuador, Bolivia, and Peru.

Under Bolívar's leadership, Colombia, Ecuador, and Venezuela formed a confederation called Gran Colombia (Greater Colombia). However, this union did not last; in 1829 Venezuela broke away from Gran Colombia under the leadership of José Antonio Páez, a mestizo who had served as a general during the war for independence from Spain. Bolívar, having seen his vision of a united South America collapse, died in *exile* in 1830, saying that his efforts had been as fruitless as having "plowed the sea."

Páez ruled for 16 relatively peaceful years. However, in 1846 General José Tadeo Monagas came to power. He established a dictatorship and ruled with his brother, José Gregorio, for the next decade.

After the Monagas brothers were forced from power in 1857, strong local leaders, called *caudillos*, fought each other for power in a struggle collectively called the Federal War. Finally, in 1870, Antonio Guzmán Blanco gained control of the country. He instituted a *despotic* regime and used his power to amass a large fortune. However, under his leadership Venezuela reduced its public debt, began building railroads, and instituted educational reforms. He retired in 1888 because of popular demonstrations against him. General Joaquín Crespo brought another brief period of peace and order between 1892 and 1899.

Oil, Profit, and Corruption

During the early decades of the 20th century, Venezuela was dominated by the caudillo Juan Vicente Gómez. He took control of the government in 1908 and ruled until his death in 1935. The dictator established good relations with foreign powers, especially the United States. Gómez invited *multinational* oil companies to develop Venezuela's vast petroleum reserves. However, he ruled Venezuela with an iron hand and used the army to brutally suppress all challenges to his regime.

After Gómez's death, the military, led by General Eleazar López Contreras, retained much power in the country. However, many Venezuelans were ready for democracy. By the 1940s, violent street demonstrations and labor strikes plagued the nation. In October 1945, a revolution broke out with riots in Caracas. A new government was set up under the presidency of a young leader, Rómulo Betancourt.

The Betancourt government brought a new approach to government. Seven of the 11 members of the *cabinet* had been educated in the United States, and all were young men. Through land reforms that broke down huge cattle ranches into small, affordable farms, and steps to lower the price of food, order was restored. A new constitution in 1947 provided for popular vote by means of a secret ballot.

Venezuela's president, Hugo Chávez, at a 2002 press conference. He has alienated many other world leaders with his fiery rhetoric. America's government considers him a threat to democracy; Chávez has accused the U.S. of trying to overthrow him. Both in and out of Venezuela, he is contro-versial: his supporters view him as an advocate for the poor, while his detractors fear that he stifles free speech.

In February 1948, the first elected president in Venezuela's history, Rómulo Gallegos, took office. Unfortunately, less than a year later Gallegos was forced from office. A military *junta* took control of Venezuela. Eventually, Marcos Pérez Jiménez emerged as sole leader of the country. His regime was as brutal as that of any of the dictators who had preceded him.

In 1958 a popular and military uprising forced Pérez Jiménez to flee the country. A democratic government was established, with Rómulo Betancourt inaugurated as president in February 1959. For the rest of the 20th century, Venezuela would be under the rule of constitutional civilian governments.

Rocky Progress

For the next 25 years, Venezuela's progress and stability depended on oil. An oil boom in the mid-1970s saw enormous wealth pour into the country—though, as always, the lower class and poor benefited little. Oil prices dropped in the late 1980s, plunging the country into crisis when hundreds of thousands of people were thrown out of work. Riots swept through Caracas and were violently repressed, and two *coup* attempts took place in 1992.

In December 1998, Venezuelans signaled their impatience with the government's inability to restore order and national pride by electing a fierce *populist*, Hugo Chávez, to the presidency with the largest vote margin in 40 years. Just six years earlier, Chávez had attempted a coup against the government, for which he had spent two years in jail. In 2000 Chávez was reelected for a six-year term, again by a comfortable margin.

But Chávez created turmoil with his *authoritarian* ways. A three-day general strike ended in a violent demonstration in April 2002, during which Chávez's snipers killed 12 people. After the incident, the military arrested Chávez. But demands by Western governments that Venezuela remain loyal to its constitution led to Chávez's reinstatement as president 48 hours later.

Chávez remained under pressure throughout the year. In December 2002 a general strike, undertaken to protest the president's policies, crippled the vital oil industry, cutting production to about one-third. Government spending curbed the strike's effects, but Venezuela stayed divided over Chávez. He was reelected for a third term in 2006, but in 2007, citizens voted against allowing him to run again.

(Opposite) Multicolored umbrellas protect vendors from the sun in this market in Mérida. (Right) A boat is anchored near a petrochemical plant at Los Taques. Oil is Venezuela's most valuable resource. The country was one of five founding members of the Organization of Petroleum Exporting Countries (OPEC), which controls about 75 percent of the world's oil reserves.

3 Boom and Bust Economy

VENEZUELA POSSESSES enormous natural resources. It is the world's fifth-largest exporter of oil, and the ninth-largest producer of oil. The national petroleum company, Venezuelan Petroleum Corporation, is the third-largest oil business in the world. Because of its mineral wealth, Venezuela is also a leading exporter of coal, iron, steel, and aluminum. On the other hand, official corruption and mismanagement have allowed the privileged class to become even richer, while a large number of Venezuelans remain poor. In the early 21st century, falling oil prices caused major economic problems, followed a few years later by a sudden surge in spending. The unpredictability of the oil market, and the inequality between the rich and poor, suggest that Venezuela needs to develop industries other than oil.

Before the Oil Boom

Spanish adventurers arrived in what is present-day Venezuela in 1498. Unable to locate precious metals or treasures, the Spaniards who came after the explorers raised cattle or collected pearls in the shallow waters near the islands off the western end of the Península de Paria. Colonial authorities organized the local Indians to grow tobacco, cotton, indigo, and cocoa. When the number of native workers declined, the Spanish throne began replacing the Indians with enslaved Africans in 1687.

Cocoa, coffee, and the desire to break away from Spain dominated the Venezuelan economy in the 18th and 19th centuries. Cocoa become more important than tobacco in the 1700s; then coffee surpassed cocoa in the 1800s. The Venezuelan war of independence devastated the economy in the early 19th century. But a coffee boom in the 1830s made Venezuela the world's third-largest exporter of coffee. Over the course of the century, the price of coffee drove the Venezuelan economy.

"Sowing the Oil"

The first commercial drilling for petroleum in Venezuela took place in 1917. By the 1920s, the long era of coffee's dominance had ended. Oil profits soon changed Venezuela from an agricultural economy into Latin America's wealthiest state.

By 1928 Venezuela was the world's leading exporter of oil and was ranked second in total petroleum production. As early as the 1930s, oil represented over 90 percent of total exports. Various social and political groups demanded better conditions for oil workers and higher taxes for oil companies. In 1936 the government launched an ambitious plan called *sembrar el petróleo*, or "sowing the oil." The idea was to plow the tremendous revenues from oil production into agriculture, industry, and society as a whole. By 1943 the government had succeeded, over the protests of the wealthy, in putting a 50 percent tax on the oil profits of foreign oil companies.

After the tax hike, money from oil spread more evenly throughout Venezuelan society. But widespread corruption and trickery by foreign companies, plus the expensive plans of military dictators, slowed down the pace of economic development. Still, the worldwide demand for oil soared throughout the 1950s and 1960s. In 1960 Venezuela became a founding member of the Organization of Petroleum Exporting Countries (OPEC). Throughout the 1960s, the government improved the standard of living by spending huge sums of money on education, health, electricity, drinkable water, and other basic services. Venezuela remained the world's leading oil exporter until 1970, the year of its peak oil production.

A Spending Spree

In 1973 world oil prices quadrupled, encouraging the largest spending spree in Venezuelan history. The government spent more money from 1974 to 1979 than it had from 1830 to 1973. During the 1970s, the government created hundreds of new state-owned businesses, which then competed with, and sometimes replaced, private companies.

Suddenly, hundreds of thousands of government jobs became available. In addition to establishing new state companies in mining, petrochemicals, and hydroelectricity, the government took over private ones. In 1975 the government *nationalized* the steel industry; the oil industry followed in 1976. Fortunes were made overnight. Upper-middle-class Venezuelans thought nothing of flying to Miami for weekend shopping trips. In 1978 and 1979, some political candidates sounded warnings about government spending. But another surge in oil prices in the years 1978–82 pushed their warnings into the background.

By the mid-1980s, however, Venezuela's economy began to unravel. Tax revenues could not equal the amount of government spending, especially after oil prices dropped by 50 percent in 1986. Venezuela stumbled into an economic crisis. By 1989 the government was forced to lay off workers, close businesses, and reduce public services.

Since the early 1990s, the country has been trying to make its economy healthier in two ways: by reducing Venezuela's debts to foreign countries and by removing price controls.

Snapshot of the Current Economy

Petroleum, which is found in the Maracaibo Basin and in the eastern part of the country, still dominates the Venezuelan economy. Crude and refined oil are the main source of government revenue. The country also is a major producer of natural gas. Venezuela has tapped its vast reserves of *bitumen* coal to produce liquid coal, a mixture of bitumen and water that is mainly used by power plants.

Other commercially mined minerals include bauxite, diamonds, gold, silver, platinum, coal, salt, copper, tin, asbestos, phosphates, titanium, and

Quick Facts: The Economy of Venezuela

Gross domestic product (GDP*):
$334.6 billion (purchasing power parity)
GDP per capita: $12,200
Inflation: 18.7%
Natural resources: petroleum, natural gas, iron ore, gold, bauxite, other minerals, hydropower, diamonds
Agriculture (3.8% of GDP): corn, sorghum, sugarcane, rice, bananas, vegetables, coffee, beef, pork, milk, eggs, fish
Industry (38.4% of GDP): petroleum, construction materials, food processing, textiles; iron ore mining, steel, aluminum; motor vehicle assembly
Services (57.8% of GDP): government, banking, tourism

Foreign trade:
Exports—$69.2 billion: petroleum, bauxite and aluminum, steel, chemicals, agricultural products, basic manufactures.
Imports—$45.5 billion: raw materials, machinery and equipment, transport equipment, construction materials.
Currency exchange rate: 2,147 bolivares = U.S. $1 (August 2008)

*GDP or gross domestic product = the total value of goods and services produced in a year.
All figures are 2007 estimates unless otherwise indicated.
Sources: CIA World Factbook 2008; Bloomberg.com

mica. Iron ore, in extensive deposits, was discovered near the Orinoco River in the 1940s. Margarita Island, off the northern coast, has enormous reserves of magnesite, a substance used by the construction industry.

Agriculture—including forestry and fishing, once the backbone of Venezuela's economy—employs about 13 percent of the workforce. The principal crops include coffee, sugarcane, maize, rice, cassava, and fruits such as bananas, plantains, and oranges. Livestock raising takes place chiefly on the llanos and east of Lake Maracaibo.

Although forests cover more than one-third of Venezuela, the timber

New vehicles are lined up outside the Ford Motors assembly plant in Valencia. In recent years the government has tried to increase Venezuela's manufacturing capacity and has welcomed multinational corporations into the country.

industry is small because few good roads reach into the deep forests. Timber is used mainly as fuel and by the building, furniture manufacturing, and paper industries.

The rich fishery resources of Venezuela include a wide variety of marine life. The most important commercial catch is shrimp, followed by tuna and sardines. Important pearl fisheries are located off Margarita Island.

Since the early 1960s, a goal of the government of Venezuela has been to increase the amount of manufacturing in the country. Ciudad Guayana, founded in 1961 in an area rich in natural resources, is now a major center for industry. After refined petroleum and related products, the leading manufactures of Venezuela include steel, aluminum, fertilizer, cement, tires, motor vehicles, processed food, beverages, clothing, and wood items.

Goods are transported throughout Venezuela on a growing network of roads. According to recent studies, Venezuela has about 59,748 miles (95,718 km) of roads, of which 34 percent are paved. The number of highways is greatest in the north-central area. New highways are being built to connect the major towns and cities. The leading seaports of Venezuela include La Guaira, Puerto Cabello, and Maracaibo. Boat transportation, especially on the Orinoco River and other rivers, has also been important.

The Road Ahead

When oil revenues rose in 2000 and 2001, the government began to pour more money into creating jobs and business opportunities. This effort stalled when world oil prices fell again in 2002. As a result, the jobless rate in Venezuela remained stubbornly high. About one in five workers had no job in 2003. By 2007, when oil prices were higher, unemployment had fallen to about 8.5 percent; the minimum wage had also increased.

Today most Venezuelans enjoy a more comfortable existence than their neighbors. Venezuela's GDP per capita, a measure of the average annual income of individuals, is $12,200, ranking 87th in the world. This figure is much higher than nearby Brazil ($9,700, ranked 105th), Colombia ($6,700, 123rd) and Guyana ($3,800; 154th). However, a sizable gap remains between Venezuela's rich and poor. Almost 40 percent of the population lives below the poverty line. And the country's increased spending power has made life more expensive for its poor.

Venezuela's wealth of oil has been both a blessing and a curse. The nation continually faces the challenge of freeing its economy from the irregular cycles of the global oil market.

(Right) The skyline of Caracas, Venezuela's capital and largest city. Caracas is considered one of the most modern cities in the world. (Opposite) A slum, or *rancho*, on the outskirts of Caracas.

5 An Urban Population

TODAY, MORE THAN 26 million people live in Venezuela. About 80 percent of the population lives in the northern highlands or coastal regions. Only about 5 percent lives in the region south of the Orinoco River, an area covering nearly 50 percent of Venezuela. The Native American population living in the jungles numbers about 50,000.

In Caracas, oil wealth has created modern buildings and a class of millionaires. But in the hills surrounding the capital city, unskilled laborers live in poverty in shantytowns. Likewise, in the countryside a small number of great landowners live in mansions, while farmworkers live in shacks and are poorly fed, diseased, and illiterate.

Caracas, the Capital

Caracas, the capital and chief city of Venezuela, is in the fertile Caracas Valley in northern Venezuela, near the Caribbean port of La Guaira. It is located at the foot of Ávila Mountain and has a year-round average temperature of about 72°F (21°C).

The city was founded in 1567 as Santiago de León de Caracas and became one of the most prosperous Spanish colonial communities in South America. It was invaded and looted by English buccaneers led by the adventurer Sir Francis Drake in 1595. In 1810, under the leadership of Simón Bolívar, it became the center of the first revolt in the war for independence from Spain (1810–21). Caracas became the capital of the Venezuelan Republic in 1829. During its history, the city has suffered several earthquakes: 12,000 people were killed and most of the city was destroyed in 1812, and 277 people were killed and many buildings collapsed or were damaged in 1967. In the years since the 1967 earthquake, metropolitan Caracas has grown from a population of 400,000 to more than 4 million inhabitants.

Today, Caracas is considered one of the most *cosmopolitan* cities of South America. The Caracas subway system is one of the most advanced in the world. The *teleférico* (cable car) takes riders to the peak of Ávila Mountain for a view of the city. The many squares and public gardens in Caracas draw tourists. One of the most popular squares is the Plaza Bolívar, named after the famous statesman and revolutionary, who was born in Caracas. The gilt-domed capitol building, the Central University of Venezuela, and the National Pantheon, where Bolívar is buried, are nearby. Another historic

Traffic rushes past the shopping district of Caracas, the commercial and industrial center of Venezuela.

building is the city cathedral, built in 1636. Caracas is the seat of the Roman Catholic archbishop of Venezuela. The National Park El Ávila has over 75,000 acres of virgin forest, which separates Caracas from the Caribbean Sea. The city has many urban parks, too. Vargas Park has a cultural complex featuring the Teresa Carreño Theater, the Museum of Contemporary Art, the Children's Museum, the National Art Gallery, and the Teatro (Theater) Ateneo de Caracas.

Other Major Cities

Maracaibo in northwestern Venezuela is the chief seaport and industrial center for the petroleum-rich Maracaibo Basin. The city is located on the western shore of a channel linking Lake Maracaibo and the Gulf of Venezuela (an arm of the Caribbean Sea). Once a village of fishing and farming huts, it became a major petroleum-shipping center with the discovery of petroleum beneath Lake

Maracaibo. Local industries produce refined petroleum, processed food, textiles, and construction materials. It is a large, heavily developed area ringed by *barrios* (shantytowns). The University of Zulia, Rafael Urdaneta University, and a museum of military history are city landmarks.

The Spanish founded Maracaibo as Nueva Zamora in 1571. Many of its buildings in the city center date from colonial times. The city prospered in the 17th century, though it was attacked several times by pirates. It lost significance until the discovery of petroleum in 1917.

Valencia in northern Venezuela is in the central highlands near Lake Valencia, on the Cabriales River. It is one of Venezuela's largest cities and main manufacturing and agricultural trade centers. Puerto Cabello, on the Caribbean Sea to the north, serves as a seaport for the city. Valencia is an important center for assembling motor vehicles. Other manufactures include chemicals, pharmaceuticals, and processed food. Among the points of interest are the narrow, Spanish-style streets of the city's old section and the large, modern bullring. The city's best-known school is the University of Carabobo. Founded by the Spanish in 1555, Valencia briefly served as Venezuela's capital in 1812 and again in 1830.

Barquisimeto in northwestern Venezuela lies on the Turbio River and on both the Pan-American and Trans-Andean highways. Agriculture is Barquisimeto's main business. Fiber bags, sandals, hammocks, leather goods, and tobacco products are manufactured in the city. Its location near a major river and two highways has helped make it a trading center for coffee, sugar, cocoa, cereals, cattle, and hides. Founded in the 16th century, the city was destroyed by an earthquake in 1812 and has been completely rebuilt.

Ciudad Guayana, formerly Santo Tomé de Guayana, is a city and industrial port in the Guiana Highlands of northeastern Venezuela where the Caroní and Orinoco Rivers meet. Founded in 1961 in an area rich in natural resources, the city quickly became a major development area, with a steel complex, two aluminum plants, a tractor factory, bauxite and gold mines, a timber reserve, and the Guri hydroelectric plant.

Maracay in northern Venezuela lies in a basin of the coastal range near the northeastern shore of Lake Valencia, southwest of Caracas. The city is a trade and industrial center and lies on a major railroad. The national airport for seaplanes is nearby on the lake. Industries include textile and paper milling, meat canning, and the manufacture of cigarettes, dairy products, apparel, perfumes, and soap. The surrounding countryside produces sugarcane, tobacco, cattle, timber, coffee, and cocoa. The city grew and prospered under Juan Vicente Gómez, who was dictator of Venezuela from 1908 until his death in 1935. Maracay is known for its agricultural and military aviation schools and centers for agriculture and veterinary research.

Ciudad Bolívar is a river port in eastern Venezuela on the *narrows* of the Orinoco River. It is a major commercial center of the Orinoco Basin. Ciudad Bolívar is known for such products as gold, diamonds, iron ore, cattle, hides, horses, rare woods, and balata, used chiefly for making golf balls and belting. The city was founded in 1764 as San Tomás de la Nueva Guayana but was popularly known as Angostura. Here in 1824 a physician first made angostura bitters, a flavoring agent used in drinks and in cooking. In the 19th century the city was briefly headquarters of the revolutionaries fighting for independence from Spain. In the 1840s, it was renamed after Simón Bolívar.

A Calendar of Venezuelan Festivals

January

In the Andean region of Táchira, Mérida, and Trujillo, **La Paradura del Niño** celebrates the birth of Jesus. A figurine of a baby in a manager is placed in the center of a large white sheet, each corner held by someone with a candle. The procession weaves through the streets at night. Spectators offer food and drink to the people in the procession as they pass by.

February

Probably the most celebrated public event of Venezuela, **Carnival** has been observed since the colonial period. The largest celebrations used to be in Caracas. But today, Carnival is not as popular in the major cities as it used to be. The coastal towns, especially El Callao, are now known for having the most spectacular celebrations.

El Callao was originally named Caratal when it was founded in 1853. In those days, it attracted foreign adventurers searching for gold. Carnival became a tradition, a chance to show off the different cultures of America, France, Britain, Spain, and Africa.

By 1925, Carnival had become an important annual event and preparations began early. Costumes, ordered from far-off shops, transformed people into kings, knights, court jesters, pirates, and other personalities. With the Caribbean islands so near, calypso dancing from Trinidad and the frilly dresses worn in Guadeloupe and Martinique became part of the show as well.

The present-day version of Carnival usually involves a parade, festivities, outdoor performances, and other events that can last several days.

March

The festival **Los Tambores de Barlovento** (The Drums of Barlovento) thunders throughout the towns of Curiepe, Higuerote, Caucagua, and Tacarigua, among others. Descendants of slaves who worked the coffee and banana plantations in colonial days celebrate their Afro-Caribbean culture. Dancers perform to the accompaniment of the drums and wooden instruments of African origin.

Los Diablos de Yare is a carnivalesque celebration. Costumed devils with human and animal faces parade through the streets of the larger towns in Venezuela, leaping and rushing at people. With crowds following behind, they arrive at the steps of local churches where they silently beg for forgiveness for their misdeeds. This pantomime originated in 16th-century Spain and was made popular by the conquistadors.

In Caracas, an international theater festival is held each year during March or April.

April

The celebration of **Semana Santa** (Holy Week) is held 40 days after Carnival, so its date can fall in late March or early April. In Venezuela, this is a solemn religious occasion, as it is in many parts of the Christian world, marking the resurrection of

A Calendar of Venezuelan Festivals

Jesus. On the morning of **Easter Sunday**, Catholic and Protestant churches swell with worshippers, many of whom spend the remainder of the day at home with family.

May

May 1 is observed as **Labor Day** in Venezuela. On the evening of May 3, worshippers with candles accompany large Christian crucifixes, decorated with flowers, to the local churches to celebrate **La Cruz de Mayo**. Traditions vary depending on the town, but often a Catholic prayer service marks the end of the procession.

June

The people of Venezuela observe June 24, the anniversary of the **Battle of Carabobo**. This important battle in 1821 freed Caracas from Spanish rule.

July

Two important holidays in this month commemorate the early days of Venezuela's history as an independent country. On July 5, **Independence Day** is celebrated, and on July 24 Venezuelans remember **Simón Bolívar's birthday**.

September

On September 4, people who work for the government of Venezuela are honored on **Civil Servants' Day**.

October

On October 12, the anniversary of Christopher Columbus's arrival in the New World in 1492, Venezuelans celebrate **Día de la Raza**.

December

Christmas (December 25) is an important time of year in Venezuela. In homes where families have erected biblical scenes of the birth of Jesus, the figure of the baby Jesus is added on Christmas Eve. On Christmas morning, many families attend Catholic Mass. People visit relatives later in the day, exchanging gifts.

Recipes

Venezuelan Black Beans and Rice

(Serves 4)
1 medium onion, chopped
1 stalk celery, diced
1 small red pepper, diced
1 cup long-grain white rice, rinsed and drained
1 1/2 cups vegetable broth
1 tsp turmeric
1 tsp oregano
1 tsp salt
1 cup egg substitute, scrambled
15 oz black beans, canned
1 tsp crushed red pepper

Directions:
1. Sauté onion 2–3 minutes; add celery, bell pepper, and rice. Cook while stirring until rice turns pale, 2–3 minutes. Reduce heat to low.
2. Add broth, turmeric, oregano, and salt. Cover and cook until rice is tender and all liquid is absorbed, 15–20 minutes. Remove from heat and fluff with fork.
3. Drain black beans, heat them, and then mix them into the rice. Top with scrambled eggs and sprinkle with crushed red pepper. Serve with lemon wedges and hot sauce.

Corn Pancakes (*Cachapas*)

3 cups frozen corn kernels (canned corn may be used)
1 tsp baking soda
1/2 to 3/4 cup milk (depending on how tender the corn is)
1/2 cup sugar
1 egg
1/2 cup regular flour
1/2 cup cornmeal

Directions:
1. Combine all the ingredients in a blender or food processor. The mix should become thick. If not, add some cornmeal.
2. Pour the mix into small pancakes approximately 1/2 inch thick and about 5 inches across on a hot skillet coated with oil or nonstick spray. Let the pancakes cook on medium heat for about one minute on each side, or until small bubbles form on the top.
3. *Cachapas* should be served hot, but they can be reheated in a microwave for 30 seconds. Put shredded white cheese, butter, or jelly on them.

Quesillo

(Serves 6)
3 1/2 cups milk
2 cans sweet condensed milk
6 eggs
3 tbsp sugar
2 tbsp vanilla extract

Directions:
1. Preheat oven at 325°F (163°C).
2. Cook sugar on stove in 2 tablespoons of water in a pan (use a round cake pan, or cookie tin, approximately 8 inches in diameter, and 3 inches deep). Watch carefully. When sugar begins to brown and thicken, set aside.
3. Beat all other ingredients in a blender.
4. Smear sugar syrup mixture to cover inside of pan, and add batter. Cover and seal pan with lid or aluminum foil.
5. Place pan in larger pot with 2 inches of water, and bring water to a boil. Put both pans in the oven—keep them together. Bake for 1 hour, and maintain 2 inches of water by adding as needed. Check for firmness by removing lid and pressing in the middle with a fork.
6. Let it cool and place in the refrigerator.
7. Turn over on plate, remove pan, slice and serve.

Guasacaca

(Serves 10–15)
1 cup chopped onions
1/4 cup green bell peppers, chopped
1/4 cup red bell peppers, chopped
3–4 garlic cloves, minced
1/2 cup vegetable oil
2 tbsp vinegar
2–3 tbsp sugar
1/4 tsp black pepper
1 tbsp chopped parsley
1 1/2 cup mashed avocado
1 1/2 cup chopped avocado
Salt (to taste)

Directions:
1. Combine first nine ingredients; then stir in mashed avocado. Finally add reserved chopped avocado and salt and stir. Refrigerate.
2. Serve in a bowl surrounded by crackers.

Glossary

alpine—typical of an elevated area, such as high mountains.

Amerindian—a Native American.

aquatic—growing or living in water.

authoritarian—relating to or favoring a political system in which obedience to the ruling person or group is strictly enforced.

bitumen—a sticky mixture of hydrocarbons derived from petroleum.

brackish—having a mixture of fresh and salt water.

cabinet—the top advisers of a president or other head of state.

caudillo—a Latin American strongman ruler, often a military figure.

conquistadors—Spanish soldier-adventurers who conquered Amerindian settlements in the Americas during the 16th century.

cosmopolitan—displaying refinement and cultivation caused by exposure to the people and cultures of many nations.

coup—the sudden overthrow of a government and seizure of political power, often by force.

despotic—exercising absolute power and authority in a tyrannical way.

exile—forced absence from one's home.

headwaters—the streams that make up the beginnings of a river.

indigenous—native to a land.

junta—a small group of people who take control of a country, ruling as a body.

multinational—operating or having investments in several countries.

Glossary

narrows—the place where a flowing body of water becomes narrower.

nationalize—to transfer a business or industry from private ownership to government control.

petroleum—an oily, flammable liquid that can be refined into such fuels as gasoline and kerosene.

populist—an advocate of the rights and interests of ordinary people.

reservation—an area of land set aside specifically for use by Native Americans.

rural—related to the countryside.

sandbar—a long ridge of sand formed by currents or tides.

savanna—a grassy, subtropical plain.

semiarid—having only light rainfall.

trade winds—winds blowing almost constantly in one direction.

tributary—a stream or creek that feeds into a larger river.

urban—having to do with a city.

Project and Report Ideas

Maps and Posters

• Create an ecology map of Venezuela. First, draw the shape of the country, adding major rivers and mountains. Then, in the margins, put pictures of the trees and animals mentioned in chapter one. Under each, write a sentence identifying and describing the item.

• Using a heavy piece of cardboard or poster board, first draw a large map of Venezuela. Then, using a mixture of flour and paste, create three-dimensional mountain ranges. Refer to a topographical map that appears in an encyclopedia as a guide. Use watercolors to paint the mountain ranges when you're finished. Be sure to label the ranges.

• Few people know how gasoline arrives at the local station. Make a poster showing the steps in drilling, extracting, and refining oil into gas.

• Create a "biography map" of Venezuela. Draw a large map of Venezuela. Leave room in the margins to write paragraph-long biographies of these key figures in Venezuelan history:

Rómulo Betancourt	Antonio Guzmán Blanco
Simón Bolívar	Christopher Columbus
Hugo Chávez	Juan Vicente Gómez
Marcos Pérez Jiménez	Diego de Losada
Alonso de Ojeda	Amerigo Vespucci

Or, on your own, research the life of Manuela Sáenz, who accompanied Simón Bolívar for eight years during his struggle to liberate Venezuela. Write a one-page report about her.

Reports and Projects

• After splitting into teams, assemble a list of the best websites for learning about Venezuela. Devise a rating system. Include a one- or two-sentence summary about the site. Combine these sites in a comprehensive guide to Venezuela on the Internet for other classes to use. (For a starting place, try **http://www.casadevenezuela.com/Englishmain.htm.**)

For More Information

Department of Commerce
14th and Constitution Ave., NW
Washington, DC 20230
Venezuela Desk: 202-482-0475
800-USA-TRADE
http://www.ita.doc.gov

Venezuela-American Chamber of Commerce
Torre Credival, Piso 10
2nda Avenida de Campo Alegre
Campo Alegre, Apartado 5181
Caracas 1010A, Venezuela
58-212-263-0833
Venam@ven.net
http://www.venamcham.org

Embassy of the Bolivarian Republic of Venezuela
1099 30th St., NW
Washington, DC 20007
(202) 342-2214
http://www.embavenez-us.org/

Venezuelan Consulate General
Seven East 51st St.
New York, NY 10022, USA
(212) 826 1660
http://www.newyork.embavenez-us.org/

Index

Index/Picture Credits

Contributors

Senior Consulting Editor **James D. Henderson** is professor of international studies at Coastal Carolina University. He is the author of *Conservative Thought in Twentieth Century Latin America: The Ideals of Laureano Gómez* (1988; Spanish edition *Las ideas de Laureano Gómez* published in 1985); *When Colombia Bled: A History of the Violence in Tolima* (1985; Spanish edition *Cuando Colombia se desangró, una historia de la Violencia en metrópoli y provincia*, 1984); and coauthor of *A Reference Guide to Latin American History* (2000) and *Ten Notable Women of Latin America* (1978).

Mr. Henderson earned a bachelor's degree in history from Centenary College of Louisiana, and a master's degree in history from the University of Arizona. He then spent three years in the Peace Corps, serving in Colombia, before earning his doctorate in Latin American history in 1972 at Texas Christian University.

Charles J. Shields is the author of 30 books for young people. He has degrees in English and history from the University of Illinois, Urbana-Champaign. Before turning to writing full-time, he was chairman of the English and guidance departments at Homewood-Flossmoor High School in Flossmoor, Illinois. He lives in Homewood, a suburb of Chicago, with his wife, Guadalupe, a former elementary school principal and now an educational consultant to the Chicago Public Schools.

ISBN 9780860375852

MUSLIM CHILDREN'S LIBRARY

HILMY THE HIPPO SERIES

HILMY THE HIPPO *Learns to Share*

Author *Rae Norridge*
Illustrator *Leigh Norridge Hodgen*
Designer *Nasir Cadir*
Co-ordinator *Anwar Cara*

Published by
The Islamic Foundation, Markfield Conference Centre
Ratby Lane, Markfield, Leicestershire, LE67 9SY, UK

T (01530) 244 944 F (01530) 244 946
E info@islamic-foundation.org.uk
  publications@islamic-foundation.com

Quran House, PO Box 30611, Nairobi, Kenya

PMB 3193, Kano, Nigeria

British Library Cataloguing in Publication Data

Norridge, Rae
    Hilmy the Hippo learns to share. – (Muslim children's library)
    1. Hilmy the Hippo (Fictitious character) – Juvenile fiction 2. Sharing
    – Juvenile fiction 3. Sharing – Religious aspects – Islam – Juvenile fiction
    4. Children's stories
    I. Title II. Hodgen, Leigh Norridge III. Islamic Foundation (Great Britain)
    823.9'2[J]

ISBN-13: 9780860375852

Printed by Proost International Book Production, Belgium

HILMY THE HIPPO

Rae Norridge

Learns to Share

Illustrated by *Leigh Norridge Hodgen*

THE ISLAMIC FOUNDATION

One bright morning, Hilmy the hippo splashed about in his waterhole. He was in a playful mood. He plunged down beneath the surface of the water and swam to the bottom. Suddenly, and to Hilmy's amazement, he saw three hippos frolicking on the floor of the waterhole.

On seeing Hilmy, the hippos swam to the surface, followed by a very angry Hilmy.

"*As-Salamu 'Alaykum,*" called Hilmy.
"*Wa-'Alaykum as-Salam,*" replied the three hippos.

"What are you doing in my waterhole?" demanded Hilmy.
"You must leave at once. This is my waterhole and I will not
share it with anyone. You must find somewhere else to live."

"Hilmy," said the large hippo. "There has been no rain for
a very long time. Our waterhole has dried up. You must be
kind to us and allow us to share this beautiful waterhole."

But Hilmy did not listen, nor did he care.
"Go away!" he shouted. "And don't come back!"
The three hippos sadly left the waterhole.

Later that day a small flock of white-faced ducks flew
down and splashed into the water.

"As-Salamu 'Alaykum," called the ducks.
"Wa-'Alaykum as-Salam," said Hilmy. "Have you come
to share this waterhole too?"

"Of course," replied one of the ducks. "There is very little water about. All the small waterholes have dried up and the river has stopped flowing. It is very sad for everyone. We must pray that it will rain soon."

Hilmy was very annoyed. He angrily shouted at the ducks. "Fly away! Find somewhere else to live. This is my waterhole!"

The white-faced ducks were frightened and flew away.

Day after day the rain did not come. Day after day the waterhole grew smaller and smaller. Soon, the waterhole was nothing but a small pool of dried mud.

Hilmy knew he needed a new place to live, so he set out to find a new waterhole.

He walked a long way across the dry savannah. Soon, he came across a colony of meerkats standing on a mound of sand.

"*As-Salamu 'Alaykum*," called one of the meerkats.
"*Wa-'Alaykum as-Salam*," replied Hilmy.
"Where are you heading, Hilmy?" asked the meerkat.

"My waterhole has dried up, so I am looking for a new place
to live," replied Hilmy.
"Why are you travelling alone, Hilmy? Have you no friends?"

"I live alone as I do not wish to share," replied Hilmy.

7

The meerkat looked at Hilmy with surprise. "We live together in large colonies, Hilmy," said the meerkat. "Without each other we would not survive. In times of need, *Insha'Allah* we are there for each other."

"Hmph," snorted Hilmy. "That is not for me."

The sun sank low on the horizon and the moon rose
up shining in a bright crescent. Bats swooped across the
night sky and owls hooted from the trees. But Hilmy did
not dally. He continued his search for a new waterhole.

When the sun rose the following day, casting a pink glow across the earth, Hilmy stopped to rest beside the lake. Hundreds and hundreds of flamingos stood feeding in the shallow water.

"*As-Salamu 'Alaykum,*" called Hilmy to the nearest flamingo.

"*Wa-'Alaykum as-Salam,*" replied the beautiful pink bird.

"There are so many of you here," said Hilmy. "How can there be enough food for everyone?"

"We live in large flocks," replied the flamingo. "We always settle where we know there is enough food for everyone. We are gregarious, that is, we like to live together."

Hilmy went on his way, leaving the flamingos to happily feed in the shallow waters of the lake.

11

Soon, he passed a small herd of zebra. Hilmy noticed that they too, were gregarious. Then he saw a group of giraffes; their heads stood tall above the trees, and Hilmy knew that they too enjoyed each other's company.

By midday, when the sun was directly overhead, Hilmy came to a large sand dune. He raced up the sandy slope, and once at the top, an amazing sight met his eyes. Before him, lay a very large expanse of water. Never before had Hilmy seen so much water. It stretched as far as the horizon.

"*Subhanallah!*" cried Hilmy. "What a wonderful sight. This is truly the largest waterhole in the world. And there is not a hippo in sight."

Hilmy ran across the white sand and splashed into the water. He had walked for so long that he was very, very thirsty. The first thing he did was to have a large gulp of water.

"*As-Salamu 'Alaykum,*" called a seagull bobbing on the waves.

"*Wa-'Alaykum as-Salam,*" replied Hilmy spitting the water from his mouth. "What is this?" he spluttered. "This water tastes of salt, I cannot drink this. I cannot live in this salty water."

"This is the sea, Hilmy, and hippos do not live in the sea." The seagull explained.

Hilmy turned to leave. He was very disappointed and he was still very, very thirsty.

15

Hilmy followed the path back to the lake where the
flamingos gathered. When he arrived, he went to quench
his thirst from the shallow water.

"*As-Salamu 'Alaykum,*" called Hilmy.
"*Wa-'Alaykum as-Salam,*" replied the flamingos. "You cannot
drink from our lake, Hilmy," they all chanted. "You must
learn a lesson. You would not share your waterhole with
others, therefore you cannot drink from our lake. When
you are prepared to share, we will share with you. Leave us
alone, Hilmy."

16

Hilmy sadly continued on his way. It was a long walk back to his waterhole. The sun beat down and there was no water to be seen.

Once again night fell and Hilmy sat down to rest for a short while. He was still very, very thirsty.

17

When morning came, Hilmy was eager to be on his way. He passed the little colony of meerkats. They stood on a mound and waved as Hilmy passed by.

Soon, Hilmy passed a small pond where the white-faced ducks had settled. At once Hilmy went over to the water's edge to have a drink.

18

"Go away, Hilmy!" shouted the white-faced
ducks. "You would not share your waterhole
with us, therefore you cannot drink our water."
With a heavy heart, Hilmy went on his way.
He was still very thirsty.

Dark clouds began to gather across the sky and thunder began to rumble in the distance. It began to rain when Hilmy reached another waterhole.

"*As-Salamu 'Alaykum*, Hilmy," called a large hippo.
"Allah in his mercy has sent the rain."

"*Wa-'Alaykum as-Salam*," replied Hilmy.
"Can I share your waterhole?"

"No," called the hippos. "You cannot share our waterhole as you did not allow us to share yours. You must go on your way. Perhaps you will learn that when others are in need you will willingly share your good fortune."

The rain splashed down as Hilmy made his way across the vast savannah.

When Hilmy reached his waterhole he saw his friend, the little chameleon, sitting on a branch. His waterhole was almost full once again.

"*As-Salamu 'Alaykum,*" called the chameleon.
"*Wa-'Alaykum as-Salam,*" replied Hilmy.

"I hope you have learnt your lesson, Hilmy," said the chameleon. "You are fortunate to have such a beautiful waterhole. We must never forget to appreciate the good times, for in life there is always a chance the good times will change. We must help and share with others when they are facing hardships."

23

Hilmy looked across at the shimmering water and the blue sky above. *Subhanallah*, he was truly blessed. He had the best waterhole in the entire world.

"*Astagfirullah*," he said quietly to himself. He had been unkind to his fellow creatures. Allah in His mercy had blessed him. Hilmy knew that it is not only a duty to share with others, it is a privilege.

GLOSSARY
of Islamic Terms

As-Salamu 'Alaykum
Literally "Peace be upon you", the traditional Muslim greeting, offered when Muslims meet each other.

Wa-'Alaykum as-Salam
"Peace be upon you too", is the reply to the greeting, expressing their mutual love, sincerity and best wishes.

Al-Hamdulillah
Literally "Praise be to Allah". It is used for expressing thanks and gratefulness to Allah. This supplication is also used when one sneezes, in order to thank Allah for having relieved discomfort out of His boundless mercy.

Subhanallah
Literally "Glory be to Allah". It reflects a Muslim's appreciation and amazement at observing any manifestation of Allah's greatness.

Insha' Allah
Literally "If Allah so wishes". Used by Muslims to indicate their decision to do something, provided they get help from Allah. It is recommended that whenever Muslims resolve to do something and make a promise, they should add "Insha' Allah".

Jazak Allah
Literally means: "May Allah Reward you" while thanking someone. A Muslim prays that Allah may reward the benefactor.

Some information about
the Animals and Birds

White-faced Ducks
White-faced ducks are related to swans. Apart from Africa, they are found in South America and Madagascar. They eat water plants.

Savannah
A savannah is a large expanse of flat land covered in grass and low vegetation.

Meerkats
Meerkats are smallish mammals that live in colonies. Sometimes there are as many as 40 in one colony. They eat insects, grubs, small mammals, scorpions and lizards.

Flamingo
Flamingos live in large colonies near water rich in salts. Their long legs are useful for wading in deep water. They eat algae and insects.